Recipes by Anne-Catherine Bley

Soups

Photographs by Akiko Ida

contents

Hot soups

Tomato and ginger

Season: all
Serves 5

1 large onion

2 garlic cloves

**2 lb ripe tomatoes
(or canned, peeled plum
tomatoes)**

1 teaspoon olive oil

**3 teaspoons grated fresh
root ginger**

2 tablespoons tomato paste

several sprigs fresh thyme

1 bay leaf

1 cup water

½ teaspoon sugar

½ cup whipping cream

**salt and freshly ground
black pepper**

Peel the onion and garlic and chop finely. Wash the tomatoes, cut in half, remove the core and seeds, and chop coarsely.

Heat the oil in a large pan; add the onion and ginger and cook over a low heat until soft. Add the garlic, tomato paste, and chopped tomato.

Tie the thyme sprigs and bay leaf together with kitchen string and add to the pan. (Leave one long piece of string and attach it to the pan handle. This makes it easy to retrieve the bundle before puréeing the soup.) Add the sugar and season with a little salt.

Add the water and bring to a boil. Lower the heat, cover and simmer gently for 15–20 minutes. Remove the herb bundle and let the soup cool a little.

Blend the soup until smooth in a blender or with a hand-held "stick" blender. Stir in the cream and adjust the seasoning to taste with salt and pepper.

Variation: Replace the ginger with 2 teaspoons curry powder.

Cream of garlic

Season: all
Serves 4–5

2 whole heads of garlic

2 cups peeled and cubed mealy potatoes

2 onions

2 tablespoons olive oil

2 cups milk

2 cups water

salt and freshly ground black pepper

An absolute promise: even after a big bowl of this soup you will be able to face your friends. Garlic from which the green shoots have been removed and which is then boiled will not leave any lingering odors on your breath.

Separate all the garlic cloves and place in a bowl of warm water to soak for a few minutes; this will make peeling easier. Split open each clove with a sharp knife and remove any green shoots; chop the garlic coarsely. Rinse the potato cubes. Peel and slice the onions.

Heat the oil in a large pan and allow the garlic to soften over a low heat for a few minutes. Add the onions to soften for 3–4 minutes more. Add the potatoes and cook for a further 2 minutes, stirring so that they do not stick.

Pour in the milk and water. Season with salt. Increase the heat slightly and simmer gently until the potatoes are cooked, around 20 minutes.

Remove from the heat and let cool a little. Blend the soup until smooth in a blender or with a hand-held "stick" blender. Season with salt and pepper to taste.

Serve piping hot, garnished with a few slices of fried garlic.

Purée of broccoli

Season: fall, winter, spring

Serves 5

13 oz broccoli

¾ cup diced carrots

1¼ cups peeled and diced mealy potatoes

4 shallots

1 tablespoon olive oil

4 cups water

salt and freshly ground black pepper

Wash the broccoli and separate into small florets. Rinse the diced carrots and potatoes. Peel and slice the shallots.

Heat the oil in a large pan, add the shallots and soften over a low heat for 5 minutes. Add the water and the broccoli, carrots, and potatoes. Season with salt and pepper. Cover and simmer gently for about 30 minutes, or until the vegetables are tender.

Remove from the heat and let cool a little. Blend the soup until smooth in a blender or with a hand-held "stick" blender. Adjust the seasoning to taste.

This soup is very creamy as it is but, if you like, stir in a spoonful of creamy yogurt or sour cream before serving.

Variation: Just before blending the soup add 8 portions of "Laughing Cow" cheese. In this case, do not add additional yogurt or sour cream.

Cream of mushroom

Season: all
Serves 4

4 shallots

**1¼ lb mushrooms (or
1 lb canned mushrooms)**

2 teaspoons olive oil

2 cups water

½ cup milk

½ cup light cream

**salt and freshly ground
black pepper**

This recipe is the proof that homemade soups are best. What's more, it's easy, straightforward (especially if you use canned mushrooms), and full of flavor.

Peel and finely slice the shallots.

Wipe the mushrooms and cut into pieces. If using canned mushrooms, drain and rinse.

Heat the oil in a large pan, add the shallots and soften over a low heat for 5 minutes. Stir in the mushrooms. Cover and cook gently for a few minutes more. Stir in the water, milk, and cream. Season with a little salt and simmer gently for 15 minutes.

Remove from the heat and let cool a little. Blend the soup until smooth in a blender or with a hand-held "stick" blender. Adjust the seasoning with salt and pepper to taste.

Pumpkin and cinnamon

Season: fall, winter, spring

Serves 5

2 lb pumpkin flesh (about 3 lb whole pumpkin)

2 onions

1 small piece fresh root ginger

1 tablespoon olive oil

2 tablespoons ground cinnamon

3 cups water

salt and freshly ground black pepper

nutmeg, to serve

Peel the pumpkin, scrape out the fibrous strands and seeds and cut the flesh into pieces.

Peel and chop the onions. Peel the ginger and chop finely.

Heat the oil in a large pan, add the onions, ginger, and half the cinnamon; cook gently over a low heat for 5 minutes to soften the onions. Add the pumpkin and cook for a further 5 minutes. Add the water, season with salt, cover, and bring to a boil. Lower the heat and simmer for 20 minutes, or until the pumpkin is very tender.

Remove from the heat and let cool a little. Blend the soup until smooth in a blender or with a hand-held "stick" blender. Adjust the seasoning with salt and pepper, and add the remaining cinnamon.

Serve piping hot, garnished with a little grated nutmeg.

Cream of pumpkin with bacon

Season: fall, winter, spring

Serves 5

2 lb pumpkin flesh (about 3 lb whole pumpkin)

2 onions

1 garlic clove

2 teaspoons olive oil

3 cups water

5 bacon slices

½ cup whipping cream

nutmeg

salt and freshly ground black pepper

Peel the pumpkin, scrape out the fibrous strands and seeds and cut the flesh into pieces. Peel and chop the onions. Soak the garlic clove in warm water for a few minutes (which makes it easier to peel), then slip off the skin and slice finely.

Heat the oil in a large pan, add the onion and garlic and cook over a low heat for a few minutes to soften. Add the pumpkin pieces and the water. Season with salt. Bring to a boil, then lower the heat and simmer gently for 25 minutes, or until the pumpkin is very tender.

Meanwhile, heat a skillet, nonstick if possible, and fry the bacon in its own fat until it is crisp. Set aside on paper towels.

Remove the soup from the heat and let cool a little. Blend the soup until smooth in a blender or with a hand-held "stick" blender. Stir in the cream, adjust the seasoning with salt and pepper and grate in a little nutmeg.

Serve piping hot with a bacon slice in each bowl.

Variation: Just before serving, add 1 or 2 avocados, cut into pieces, instead of the bacon slices.

Cream of squash

Season: fall
(October–December)
Serves 6

2 lb squash

2 onions

2 teaspoons olive oil

4 cups water

nutmeg

salt and freshly ground
black pepper

Squash is very similar to pumpkin and there are many different varieties. I prefer very small squash, with a very deep orange, almost red color. These are only available in season, so try your local farmer's market if you can't find any in the supermarket.

Scrub the squash well but do not peel unless the skin is very tough. Cut in half and remove the seeds and any stringy, fibrous bits; cut the the flesh of squash into pieces. Peel and chop the onions.

Heat the oil in a large pan; add the onion and cook over a low heat for a few minutes to soften. Add the squash and the water. Season with salt. Bring to a boil, then lower the heat and simmer gently until the squash is very tender, about 20 minutes.

When cooked, remove from the heat and let cool a little. Blend the soup until smooth in a blender or with a hand-held "stick" blender. Grate in a little nutmeg and adjust the seasoning with salt and pepper.

Serve hot.

Variation: This soup has a slight chestnut flavor and is delicious just as it is, but you could stir in a swirl of light cream, or sour cream, just before serving.

Chickpea with Eastern spices

Season: all
Serves 6

1½ cups canned chickpeas (garbanzo beans)

1¼ lb ripe tomatoes (or canned peeled plum tomatoes)

1 bunch flatleaf parsley

2 onions

3 garlic cloves

1 tablespoon olive oil

1½ teaspoons curry powder

1½ teaspoons ground cumin

2 cups water

large handful raisins

salt and freshly ground black pepper

Rinse and drain the chickpeas. Wash the tomatoes, cut in half and remove the core and seeds. Cut the flesh into pieces. Wash the parsley and strip off the leaves. Peel and chop the onions and garlic. (Soak the garlic in water for a few minutes to make peeling easier.)

Heat the oil in a large pan, add the spices and cook over a low heat for a minute or two. Add the garlic and onions and cook for a further 5 minutes to soften. Stir in the tomatoes, chickpeas, and parsley. Pour in the water and season with salt. Cover and cook over low heat for 30 minutes.

Remove from the heat and let cool a little. Pulse in the blender or with a hand-held "stick" blender to obtain a coarse texture soup, to your taste. Return to the pan, add the raisins and cook for 5 minutes more before serving.

Cauliflower and leek

Season: spring,
summer, fall
Serves 4

1 onion

1 small leek

12 oz cauliflower

2 teaspoons olive oil

2 cups milk

1 cup water

salt and freshly ground
black pepper

I have never been a great fan of cauliflower, unless it comes baked and smothered in a creamy cheese sauce, but this recipe has made me a convert.

Peel and chop the onion. Trim the leek, cut into thin slices and rinse well. Separate the cauliflower into small florets and rinse in a colander.

Heat the oil in a large pan and add the onion and leek. Cover and cook over a low heat for a few minutes to soften. Add the cauliflower, milk, and water. Season with salt, cover and bring to a boil. Lower the heat and simmer gently for 10–15 minutes.

Remove from the heat and let cool a little. Blend the soup until smooth in a blender or with a hand-held "stick" blender. Adjust the seasoning with salt and pepper to taste.

This soup is especially delicious served with crusty bread.

Variation: This soup is creamy on its own, but you could add some grated cheese, according to taste.

Cauliflower with cumin seeds

Season: spring,
summer, fall

Serves 6

1 lb cauliflower

1 onion

2 teaspoons olive oil

1 teaspoon cumin seed

2 cups milk

2 cups water

**salt and freshly ground
black pepper**

**½ teaspoon cumin seeds,
to serve**

Separate the cauliflower into florets and rinse in a colander. Peel and chop the onion.

Heat the oil in a large pan, add the 1 teaspoon cumin seeds and cook for 1–2 minutes, taking care not to let the seeds burn. Add the onion and cook over a low heat until soft and translucent. Add the cauliflower, milk, and water. Season with salt to taste. Bring to a boil, lower the heat and simmer gently for 10–15 minutes.

Remove from the heat and let cool a little. Blend the soup until smooth in a blender or with a hand-held "stick" blender. Adjust the seasoning with salt and pepper to taste.

Sprinkle with the ½ teaspoon cumin seeds before serving.

Split pea with bacon

Season: fall, winter,
spring
Serves 6

3 cups thinly sliced leeks

1 cup diced carrots

2 onions

1½ cups dried split peas

1 tablespoon olive oil

6 cups water

a few fresh thyme sprigs

1 bay leaf

2 thick-cut smoked bacon slices

salt and freshly ground black pepper

This is a very thick and filling soup, the ideal comfort food for winter.

Rinse the leeks and carrots. Peel and cut the onions into small dice. Rinse the split peas in cold running water, picking out any that are discolored.

Heat the oil in a large pan; add the onions and leeks and soften over a low heat for 5 minutes, stirring often. Add the water and bring to a boil.

Tie the thyme sprigs and bay leaf together with kitchen string. (Leave one long piece of string and attach it to the pan handle, which makes it easy to retrieve the bundle before puréeing the soup.) Stir in the split peas and carrots and season lightly with salt and pepper. Lower the heat, cover and simmer gently for 30–40 minutes, stirring occasionally.

Meanwhile, cut the bacon slices into small pieces. Brown the bacon in its own fat in a nonstick skillet until crisp. Set aside on paper towels.

When the peas are tender, remove the herb bundle and let the soup cool a little. Blend the soup until smooth in a blender or with a hand-held "stick" blender. Taste for seasoning, having first checked the bacon pieces for saltiness.

Serve piping hot, garnished with the crispy bacon pieces.

Lentil with cilantro

Season: all
Serves 6

3 cups French green lentils (lentilles du Puy)

2 onions

2 tablespoons olive oil

8 cups water

4 tablespoons lemon juice

salt and freshly ground black pepper

1 bunch of fresh cilantro and a few fresh mint sprigs, to serve

Lentils are the easiest pulse to cook. Even though the cooking time is a bit long, this is the only inconvenience as the resulting dish is well worth the wait.

Rinse the lentils according to instructions on the packet, they do not need presoaking. Peel the onions and chop finely.

Heat 1 tablespoon of the oil in a large pan, add the onions and cook over a low heat, stirring occasionally, until soft. Stir in the lentils and water. Season with salt and simmer gently for 45 minutes, or until the lentils are tender.

Stir in the lemon juice and remaining olive oil. Remove from the heat and blend the soup until smooth in a blender or with a hand-held "stick" blender. Season with salt and pepper to taste.

Chop the cilantro and mint finely. Sprinkle over the soup just before serving.

Lentil with spicy sausage

Season: fall, winter, spring
Serves 8

400 g (13 oz) French green lentils (*lentilles du Puy*)

1 onion

1 carrot

1 teaspoon olive oil

8 cups water

1 French-style cooking sausage (saucisse de Morteau, or if unavailable use Toulouse sausage, or chorizo for a stronger flavor)

1 bouquet garni

salt and freshly ground black pepper

Rinse the lentils according to the instructions on the packet, they do not need presoaking. Peel the onions and chop finely. Peel and slice the carrot into rounds.

Heat the oil in a large pan, add the onion and cook over a low heat, stirring occasionally, until soft. Add the carrot and lentils and mix well.

Pour in the water. Add the sausage whole and the bouquet garni (tied to the pan handle for easy removal). Season lightly with salt.

Bring to a boil, then lower the heat and simmer gently for 45 minutes. When the lentils are cooked, remove from the heat and take out the bouquet garni and the sausage. Set the sausage aside and keep warm.

Blend the soup until smooth in a blender or with a hand-held "stick" blender. Remove the skin from the sausage, slice into thick rounds and cut each round into quarters. Adjust the seasoning, having first checked the flavor of the sausage.

Stir in the sausage pieces and serve the soup piping hot.

Celery root with blue cheese

Season: fall, winter, spring
Serves 6

1 celery root

2 onions

2 teaspoon olive oil

4 cups water

4 oz blue cheese

salt and freshly ground black pepper

Peel the celery root and cut into small pieces. Peel the onions and chop finely.

Heat the oil in a large pan, add the onions and cook over a low heat, covered, until softened but without browning, stirring occasionally. Add the celery root, pour in the water and season with salt.

Cover and bring to a boil, then lower the heat and simmer gently until the celery root is tender, about 25 minutes.

Remove from the heat and crumble in two-thirds of the cheese. Blend the soup until smooth in a blender or with a hand-held "stick" blender. Adjust the seasoning with salt and pepper to taste, having first checked the cheese for saltiness.

Cut the remaining cheese into small pieces and add to the soup just before serving.

Variation: Crunchy croutons make an excellent addition to this soup. You can find out how to make them on page 48.

Chestnut with bacon bits

Season: winter
Serves 8

1 carrot

1 celery stalk

1 onion

2 garlic cloves

2 teaspoons olive oil

1¼ lb whole peeled chestnuts, canned or vacuum packed

1 bouquet garni

6 cups water

12-oz piece of smoked bacon

salt and freshly ground black pepper

Chestnuts lend a slightly sweet taste to this soup, which is pleasantly balanced by the saltiness of the bacon.

Peel the carrot and cut into rounds. Wash the celery, trim any leaves and slice thinly. Peel and chop the onion and garlic. (Soak the garlic for a few minutes in water to make the peeling easier.)

Heat the oil in a large pan; add the carrot, onion, celery, and garlic. Cook over a low heat, stirring occasionally, for 5 minutes to soften. Rinse the chestnuts. Add to the vegetables, along with the bouquet garni and the water.

Season with salt and bring to a boil. Lower the heat, cover and cook for 40 minutes. When the chestnuts are tender, remove the bouquet garni. Remove the soup from the heat and blend until smooth in a blender or with a hand-held "stick" blender.

Adjust the seasoning with salt and pepper but go lightly with the salt, since the bacon adds saltiness as well.

Cut the bacon into small pieces and fry in their own fat until golden and crispy. Stir into the soup just before serving.

Note: Peeled chestnuts in cans or vacuum packed are sometimes difficult to find outside the Christmas period. They are preferable because preparing fresh chestnuts is a lengthy process: the hard outer skin must first be peeled, then the chestnuts boiled so that the inner skins can be removed more easily.

Cream of mixed greens with chorizo

Season: spring
Serves 6

1 lb fresh spinach

4 oz fresh sorrel

4 oz young dandelion leaves

2 shallots

1 tablespoon olive oil

5 cups water

1 small chorizo

pinch of grated nutmeg

salt and freshly ground black pepper

Separately wash and trim all the greens. Peel and chop the shallots finely.

Heat the oil in a large pan, add the shallots and cook over a low heat for 5 minutes to soften. Add the greens and cook for a few minutes more. Add the water and season with salt. Cover and simmer gently for 30 minutes.

Meanwhile, slice the chorizo into rounds. Fry in a hot nonstick skillet in their own fat for a few minutes then set aside to drain on paper towels. Keep warm.

Remove the soup from the heat, let cool a little, then blend until smooth in a blender or with a hand-held "stick" blender. Add the grated nutmeg and adjust the seasoning with salt and pepper to taste.

Add the chorizo slices just before serving.

Note: If young dandelion leaves are unavailable, use extra sorrel, which will make the soup quite tart. Other greens can also be used, such as young nettle tips, radish, or turnip greens.

Spring is the best time for sourcing a good variety of greens. This is when dandelion leaves are at their best – once they have flowered, they are no longer suitable for consumption. However, do not pick from roadside verges.

Be sure to wash all greens well, in plenty of water.

The uncooked amount of greens may seem a lot but the volume will reduce significantly when cooked. Be sure to choose a very large pan to accommodate the quantities.

Cabbage with smoked haddock

Season: spring,
early summer
Serves 8

1³/₄ lb kale, or new season
spring cabbage hearts.

2 cups diced waxy
potatoes

1¹/₂ cups diced carrots

2 garlic cloves

5 cups water

1 smoked haddock fillet,
skinned

salt and freshly ground
black pepper

Finely shred the kale or spring cabbage hearts and discard the core or any coarse stems. Rinse the diced potatoes and carrots. Peel the garlic and slice thinly.

Pour the water into a large pan and add the diced potato and sliced garlic. Season lightly with salt. Bring to a boil, then lower the heat and simmer gently, covered, for 10 minutes. Add the shredded kale, or cabbage, and diced carrots. Cook for about a further 10 minutes.

Meanwhile, prepare the smoked haddock. Remove any traces of skin and any bones. Cut into small pieces. and set aside.

The vegetables are ready when the potatoes are beginning to disintegrate and the carrots are tender. Remove from the heat at this point.

Blend in a blender or with a hand-held "stick" blender to obtain a coarse texture. Adjust the seasoning but take care not to oversalt as the smoked haddock is salty. Stir in the pieces of raw fish just before serving.

Note: If preferred, the smoked haddock fillet can be lightly poached in milk, then flaked and added to the soup just before serving.

Carrot and cilantro

Season: all
Serves 6–7

2 lb carrots

1 lb onions

2 tablespoons olive oil

1/2 teaspoon ground coriander

4 cups water

1/2 cup sour cream, or creamy yogurt

1 bunch fresh cilantro

salt and freshly ground black pepper

This soup is at its best in the spring or early summer when carrots are young and tender.

Peel the carrots and slice into rounds. Peel and chop the onions finely.

Heat the oil in a large pan and add the onions and ground coriander. Cook over a low heat until the onions have softened, about 5 minutes. Add the carrots and mix well. Stir in the water and season with salt.

Bring to a boil, then lower the heat and simmer gently until the carrots are tender, about 20–30 minutes. Remove from the heat and let cool a little. Blend the soup until smooth in a blender or with a hand-held "stick" blender. Adjust the seasoning with salt and pepper to taste and stir in the sour cream or yogurt.

Chop the cilantro leaves finely and add to the soup just before serving.

Carrot and coconut milk

Season: all

Serves 8

3 lb carrots

1 small bunch scallions, or salad onions

6 cups water

1 teaspoon ground coriander

1 teaspoon ground cumin

1 teaspoon ground cinnamon

1 cup coconut milk

salt and freshly ground black pepper

Peel the carrots and slice into rounds. Peel and finely chop the white bulb of the scallions. Discard the green tails or chop finely and use as a garnish.

Pour the water into a large pan and add the carrot slices. Season with salt, bring to a boil, lower the heat and cook for about 20–30 minutes or until the carrots are very tender.

Remove from the heat and stir in the spices, chopped scallions and the coconut milk. Blend the soup until smooth in a blender or with a hand-held "stick" blender. Adjust the seasoning with salt and pepper to taste.

Note: This soup can also be served chilled.

Pea with mint

Season: all
Serves 6

4½ cups shelled fresh peas (about 4½ lb pods)

4 salad onions, or small bunch of scallions

2 Little Gem, or small romaine, lettuces

4 cups water

⅔ cup whipping cream

2 fresh mint sprigs

salt and freshly ground black pepper

Fresh new season peas and large salad onions make this soup just divine. When these are not available, use frozen peas and 2 small ordinary onions.

Shuck the peas. Peel and slice the white bulbs of the onions. Wash the lettuce and shred coarsely.

Pour the water into a large pan and add the peas, onions, and lettuce. Add a little salt, bring to a boil, then lower the heat and simmer gently for 15–20 minutes or until all the vegetables are tender.

Remove from the heat and stir in the cream and the leaves from the mint sprigs. Blend the soup until smooth in a blender or with a hand-held "stick" blender. Adjust the seasoning with salt and pepper and serve.

Variation: This soup is also delicious served chilled and makes a delightful appetizer for a summer dinner party. Serve in small dishes with a dollop of sour cream.

Zucchini and creamy cheese

Season: spring,
summer, fall
Serves 4–5

2 lb zucchini

**3 large salad onions, or
small bunch of scallions**

2 cups water

pinch of ground cumin

**8 portions "Laughing Cow"
cheese**

**salt and freshly ground
black pepper**

Another very easy recipe! The creamy texture of the cheese blends well with the zucchini. This will be a guaranteed hit with children.

Wash the zucchini, then trim the ends and slice into rounds. Rinse the onions and cut the white bulbs into quarters.

Pour the water into a large pan and add the zucchini, onions, ground cumin, and a little salt. Bring to a boil, then lower the heat and cook for 15 minutes, or until the zucchini are tender.

Remove from the heat, add the cheese and blend the soup until smooth in a blender or with a hand-held "stick" blender. Adjust the seasoning with salt and pepper to taste.

Note: Zucchini give off liquid when cooked and this can produce too much broth. Before blending, remove some of the liquid. If the blended soup is too thick, dilute with the reserved broth as needed.

Nettle soup

Season: spring
Serves 5

2 onions

1 lb nettles

1½ cups diced mealy potatoes

1 tablespoon olive oil

4 cups water

⅔ cup whipping cream

salt and freshly ground black pepper

This old-fashioned country soup is currently enjoying an urban revival. The main problem is obtaining the nettles; I have painful memories of stinging hands, despite using thick gloves.

Peel and chop the onions finely. Rinse the nettles thoroughly. Rinse the potatoes.

Heat the oil in a large pan, add the onions and soften over a low heat for 5 minutes. Add the nettles and cover. As soon as the nettles have wilted, add the potatoes and the water. Season with a little salt. Bring to a boil, then lower the heat and simmer gently for 20 minutes.

Remove from the heat and let cool a little. Blend the soup until smooth in a blender or with a hand-held "stick" blender. Adjust the seasoning with salt and pepper to taste. Swirl in the cream just before serving.

Note: Choose only the youngest nettle shoots – the best time to find these is in April–May. Do not pick from anything taller than 12–14 inches, and only remove up to about 4 inches of the tips. Avoid any flowering stalks, as these are not suitable for consumption.

Choose only nettles from a site that has not been subjected to any chemical sprays, such as your own yard or a wild area. Avoid any growing next to crops as these are generally sprayed, especially grains, which are often over-treated. Remember to wear thick kitchen or gardening gloves.

Gazpacho

Season: summer
Serves 8

4 onions

2 garlic cloves

1 green, or yellow, bell pepper

1 cucumber

3 lb ripe tomatoes (or canned peeled plum tomatoes)

1/2 teaspoon sugar

3 tablespoons olive oil

3 tablespoons balsamic vinegar

3/4 cup water

few dashes Tabasco

For the croutons:

1 slice of bread per person

2 tablespoons olive oil

This is surely the most well-known, and well-loved, chilled soup. There are many variations to the authentic version from the Andalusian region of Spain; this recipe is my favorite. It is an explosion of fresh flavors, made even more appealing because the texture of crunchy, crisp vegetables is retained.

Peel the onions and garlic, and chop finely. Wash all the other vegetables. Seed the pepper and cut into thin slices. Cut the cucumber into small dice but do not peel. If the skin is very thick, peel alternating slices lengthways from the cucumber, as it is important to put as much green color into the soup as possible. Cut the tomatoes in half and remove the core and seeds before coarsely chopping the flesh.

Put all the vegetables in a large bowl. Add the sugar, olive oil, and balsamic vinegar. Season to taste with salt and pepper, and mix well.

Briefly blend the soup in a blender or with a hand-held "stick" blender, adding water as necessary to thin slightly; the mixture should not be smooth. Adjust the seasoning with salt and pepper, also adding more vinegar or Tabasco according to taste. Refrigerate for at least 1 hour before serving.

For the croutons: Cut the bread into small cubes and let stand to dry out. Heat the oil gently in a skillet. Add the cubes of bread and cook, stirring often, until evenly browned. Serve separately with the soup. These can be made up to 1 day in advance.

Summer chilled beet

Season: summer
Serves 5

6 medium raw beets

8 shallots

4 cups water

juice of 3 oranges and grated rind of 1 orange

2 teaspoons sugar

2 tablespoons balsamic vinegar

²/₃ cup sour cream, to serve

salt and freshly ground black pepper

This is as much a pleasure to behold as it is to eat.

Peel the beets and cut into dice. Peel the shallots and chop finely. Put the water into a large pan, add the shallots and beets and bring to a boil. Lower the heat and simmer gently for 30 minutes or until the beets are tender.

Remove from the heat and add the orange juice and sugar. Blend the soup until smooth in a blender or with a hand-held "stick" blender. Stir in the vinegar and season with salt and pepper to taste. Stir in the orange zest. Refrigerate for at least 1 hour before serving.

Top with a dollop of sour cream just before serving.

Chilled cucumber with mint

Season: summer
Serves 4

1 cucumber

2 tomatoes

1 celery stalk

3–4 fresh mint sprigs, plus a few for garnish

1 garlic clove

1 cup milk

salt and freshly ground black pepper

Wash all the vegetables. Do not peel the cucumber; if the skin is very thick, peel only alternating slices lengthways. Cut the cucumber into small dice. Halve the tomatoes and remove the core and seeds before cutting the flesh into dice. Remove any stringy bits from the celery and chop finely. Wash the mint, pat dry with paper towels and strip the leaves from the stems.

Peel the garlic and crush over a large bowl. Add all the vegetables and pour in the milk. Season with salt and pepper.

Blend the soup until smooth in a blender or with a hand-held "stick" blender, adding a little water if necessary. Refrigerate until needed for at least 1 hour, and serve well chilled.

Serve garnished with a sprig of mint, adding ice if not sufficiently chilled.

Chilled cream of zucchini with curry

Season: summer
Serves 4–5

2 lb zucchini

1 garlic clove

1 onion

1 tablespoon olive oil

2 teaspoons curry powder

2 cups water

1 cup plain creamy yogurt
(not the set kind)

salt and freshly ground
black pepper

Wash the zucchini and cut into pieces. Peel the garlic and onion and chop finely. Heat the oil in a pan, add the garlic and onion and cook gently over low heat until soft. Stir in the curry powder and cook for a few more minutes. Add the zucchini and the water. Season with a little salt.

Cook until the zucchini pieces are tender, about 15 minutes. Remove from the heat and let cool a little. Blend the soup until smooth in a blender or with a hand-held "stick" blender. Chill in the refrigerator.

When the soup is completely chilled, stir in the yogurt as required. Adjust the seasoning with salt and pepper to taste and return to the refrigerator. Serve very well chilled.

Chilled spinach and avocado

Season: spring, summer
Serves 6

1 lb fresh spinach

2 onions

1 teaspoon olive oil

2 cups water

2 cups milk

2 avocados

juice of 1 lime

1 cup Greek-style thick yogurt

grated nutmeg

2 teaspoons Worcestershire, or soy, sauce

salt and freshly ground black pepper

Wash the spinach leaves thoroughly. Peel and chop the onions.

Heat the oil in a large pan, add the onions and cook over a low heat until the onions have softened. Stir in the spinach and let the leaves wilt for a few minutes. Add the water and milk and season with a little salt. Cover and simmer gently for 15 minutes.

Remove from the heat and let cool a little. Blend the soup until smooth in a blender or with a hand-held "stick" blender. Chill in the refrigerator for at least 2 hours.

Peel the avocados, cut into pieces and toss with the lime juice to avoid discoloring.

When the spinach mixture is chilled, add the avocado and yogurt and blend again until smooth. Stir in a pinch of grated nutmeg and season with the Worcestershire, or soy, sauce. Refrigerate for at least a further 1 hour.

Note: Summer is the best time for fresh spinach, but frozen can be used if fresh is not available.

Vichyssoise

Season: spring, summer
Serves 6

1 lb trimmed leeks, white part only

1 lb mealy potatoes

1 onion

1 tablespoon olive oil

1½ cups water

¾ cup milk

⅔ cup whipping cream

salt and freshly ground white pepper

1 small bunch of fresh chives, finely snipped, to serve

The traditional color for Vichyssoise is white, so retrim the leeks and discard any remaining green parts. Thinly slice the white part and wash well. Peel the potatoes, cut into pieces and rinse. Peel and chop the onion.

Heat the oil in a large pan, add the onion and soften over a low heat, covered, for 5 minutes, checking regularly to make sure the onions are not browning – to keep the soup as white as possible. Stir in the leeks, then cover and cook for a further 5 minutes, again checking constantly to make sure the vegetables are not browning.

Add the potatoes and the water. Season with a little salt, then cover and simmer gently until the vegetables are tender, about 25 minutes. Skim off any foam that rises to the surface. Stir in the milk and cook for a further 5 minutes.

Remove from the heat and let cool a little. Blend the soup until completely smooth in a blender or with a hand-held "stick" blender. Adjust the seasoning with salt and white pepper to taste. Let cool at room temperature for 1 hour, then refrigerate until completely chilled – for at least 1 hour.

Just before serving, stir in the cream and mix well. Serve well chilled, garnished with the snipped chives.

Chocolate butter cake

Serves 8

3 eggs

½ cup sugar

scant cup all-purpose flour

7 oz best quality Continental dark chocolate (70% cocoa solids)

⅔ cup water

4 oz butter

What is a chocolate cake doing in a collection of soup recipes? Well, a bowl of tasty soup followed by a piece of delicious chocolate cake is a meal in itself – at lunchtime, at anytime. Treat yourself – you deserve it!

Preheat the oven to 400°F. Butter a loaf pan.

In a large bowl, beat together the eggs and the sugar. Add the flour and continue beating until thoroughly blended. Set to one side.

Break the chocolate into small pieces and place in a microwave-proof bowl. Microwave for 2 minutes to melt. (Alternatively, melt the pieces in a bowl over a pan of barely simmering water. Do not let the bowl touch the water.)

Add the water to the melted chocolate and stir well. Cut the butter into small pieces and add to the chocolate mixture. Microwave for 1–2 minutes more, or replace over the simmering water, until the butter is melted, then remove and stir well.

Add the combined melted chocolate and butter to the egg mixture and mix well.

Pour the batter into the greased loaf pan and bake for 15 minutes. The cake should not be completely cooked through; a skewer inserted in the middle should not come out clean.

Allow to stand 15 minutes before turning out the cake.

Spiced sweet cream of carrot and coconut milk

Season: all
Serves 4

4 medium carrots

⅔ cup milk

⅔ cup water

½ teaspoon ground coriander

1 teaspoon ground cinnamon

4 pinches ground nutmeg

⅔ cup coconut milk

⅔ cup sweetened condensed milk

few drops vanilla extract

1½ tablespoons unsweetened desiccated coconut

This recipe was created by one of my chefs, Fritz Talvin. Carrot and coconut milk soup (see page 40) makes a frequent appearance and one day he got the idea to try a sweet version. It's a good thing he did; it is delicious, and evokes Indian desserts, slightly mysterious and also made from carrots.

Peel the carrots and slice into rounds.

Pour the milk and water into a large pan and stir in the coriander, cinnamon, and nutmeg. Cook over a low heat until the carrots are tender, about 30 minutes.

Remove from the heat and stir in the coconut milk, sweetened condensed milk, and the vanilla extract. Blend the soup until smooth in a blender or with a hand-held "stick" blender; the mixture should be very creamy.

Stir in the desiccated coconut and let cool to room temperature. Refrigerate for at least 1 hour before serving.

Serve well chilled, sprinkled with a little desiccated coconut.

© Hachette Livre (Marabout) 2003
This edition published in 2004 by Hachette Illustrated UK, Octopus Publishing Group
Ltd., 2–4 Heron Quays, London E14 4JP

English translation by JMS Books LLP (email: moseleystrachan@blueyonder.co.uk)
Translation © Octopus Publishing Group Ltd.

A CIP catalog for this book is available from the Library of Congress

ISBN: 1-84430-109-5

Printed by Tien Wah, Singapore